A ROOKIE BIOGRAPHY

KATHERINE DUNHAM

Black Dancer

By Carol Greene

CHILDRENS PRESS®

CHICAGO

This book is for Pat and Fred McKissack.

Katherine Dunham

Library of Congress Cataloging-in-Publication Data

Greene, Carol.
    Katherine Dunham : Black dancer / by Carol Greene.
      p.   cm. — (Rookie biography)
    Includes index.
    Summary: Presents the personal experiences and professional
achievements of the black dancer, choreographer, and founder of the
Dunham Dance Company.
    ISBN 0-516-04252-1
    1. Dunham, Katherine—Juvenile literature. 2. Dancers—United
States—Biography—Juvenile literature. [1. Dunham, Katherine.
2. Dancers. 3. Choreographers. 4. Afro-Americans—Biography.] I. Title.
II. Series: Greene, Carol. Rookie biography.
GV1785.D82G74   1992
792.8′028′092—dc20
[B]   92-8769
                                              CIP
                                              AC

Katherine Dunham
is a real person.
She was born in 1910.
She was a great dancer
and has taught people
all over the world
about black dancing.
This is her story.

TABLE OF CONTENTS

Chapter 1   Many Homes................... 5
Chapter 2   Dancing and Learning......... 13
Chapter 3   Dancing and Traveling 23
Chapter 4   Dancing and Hurting.......... 33
Chapter 5   Another Home 39
Important Dates 46
Index.................................... 47

Chapter 1

Many Homes

The room was warm
and bright and
full of music.
In it were the people
Katherine loved best.

Father and Mother
were making the music.
Brother Albert listened.
So did Katherine.
She felt safe and happy.

Katherine Dunham's
mother with
brother Albert

But those good times
did not last long.
Katherine's mother died
when Katherine was three.

Her father sent her
and Albert to live
with Aunt Lulu in Chicago.
There Cousin Irene
took Katherine to see
shows at the theater.

She saw singing
and dancing, funny people,
and beautiful clothes.
Katherine loved that.

But sometimes she felt
hungry and cold.

Then Katherine and Albert
went to live with
other relatives.
The children in that family
were not kind to them.

One day, Katherine's father
took his children home.
He had a new business
in Joliet, Illinois.
He had a new wife, too.
She was a kind woman
named Annette.

Annette Dunham

Katherine Dunham at age seven

Katherine felt safe
and happy again.

The whole family worked
in the dry-cleaning business,
even little Katherine.
But she went to school, too.

Katherine and her friends
liked to put on shows.
Katherine made sure
the shows had a lot
of singing and dancing.

Later, Katherine started
a secret club at school,
the Eagle Eye Society.
The girls in the club
wore bright red headbands
with a big eye on them.

Katherine was happy again when she moved to Joliet, Illinois.

Now Katherine wanted
just one more thing
—dancing lessons.

Her father thought
she was silly.
He didn't want to
spend the money.
But he did it.
And Katherine danced.

Katherine Dunham at age sixteen

Chapter 2

Dancing and Learning

In high school, Katherine
took dance classes.
She joined a dance club.
She played sports.
High school was fun.

But at home,
her family had problems.
Her father thought only
about business and money.
He wanted everyone
to work all the time.

One day, he got into
a fight with Albert.
Albert left home.
He would go to
college in Chicago.
Katherine missed him.

Albert Dunham,
Katherine's brother

Then Annette left, too.
Katherine didn't want
to stay alone with
her crabby father.
So she went with Annette.

Downtown Chicago looked like this when Albert and Katherine went to college.

"Come to Chicago,"
Albert kept telling her.
"Go to college here.
I'll help you."

At last Katherine did it.
She took college classes
and worked at a library.
The people at the library
made her work and eat alone
because she was black.

15

Katherine
Dunham
at age
eighteen

That was bad.
But Katherine found
many good things
in Chicago, too.

She acted in a theater
and, of course,
she took dancing lessons.

Then Albert got married
and moved out of town.
Katherine felt all alone.
So she danced harder.
Dancing always made
her feel better.

Katherine (left) with her brother Albert's wife

Young students at Katherine's dance school in 1938

"Why don't you start
a dancing school?"
asked her friends.
Katherine did.

She thought black dancing
was special, and
that's what she taught.
She made up dances, too.

The school didn't last long.
It had money problems.
But it was good for Katherine.

She kept thinking
about black dancing.
She learned that some
American dances were much
like dances in Africa.
That was exciting.

Katherine started more schools.
She danced in a ballet.
But she couldn't stop
thinking about black dancing
and how it went back
to dances in Africa.

Katherine wanted to
learn more about that.

Katherine Dunham's dance group performing a dance
like the ones that Katherine learned in Haiti

Chapter 3

Dancing and Traveling

Katherine took classes
about black countries.
But she really wanted
to visit them and
see the people dance.

At last she got money
to visit some islands
in the West Indies.

Katherine went to
four different islands.
She liked Haiti best.
People there liked her.
They told her and
showed her many things.

23

They even let Katherine
dance with them.
She never forgot that dance.

After her trip, Katherine knew
more about black dancing.
She also learned something
important about herself.
She wanted to dance
—all the time.

John Pratt and Katherine Dunham

So Katherine started her own
group of black dancers.
Her new husband, John Pratt,
helped her with the group.

Katherine (bottom center) dancing in "Carnival of Rhythm"

They danced all around
the state of Illinois.
Some of their dances were
like those in the islands.
People loved them.

Then Katherine and John
moved to New York City.
The Dunham Dance Company
put on a show there.
It was a big hit.

Times Square, New York City, in 1943

Katherine with partner Tommy Gomez,
dancing in a show called "Tropical Revue"

Many of Katherine's dances were based
on the dances of the West Indian islands.

Soon people all across
the country wanted to
see Katherine's group.

All of her dancers were
full of life and energy.
But Katherine's own dancing
was like an explosion.
People couldn't believe it.

The group liked traveling
and putting on shows.
But it was hard work, too.
In some places, people
were mean to them
because they were black.

That made Katherine mad.
She tried to make
those unkind people change.
Sometimes they did.

Katherine dancing in a show on New York's Broadway

And most of the time,
Katherine was happy.
She really was
a dancer now
—a great dancer.

Katherine leading her dance group in a practice session

Chapter 4

Dancing and Hurting

Dancing does not last forever.
As time went by,
Katherine's body began
to hurt from arthritis.
She had two operations
on her knees.

So she started a new
school in New York.
She taught dancing.
Her students also learned
how to get along
with different people.

Still, Katherine had to
go on dancing too,
even when it hurt.
She needed the money
for her school.

She took her company
to Mexico, Europe,
and Latin America.
People cheered for them.

Katherine and her
dance company arriving
in Paris, France, on
their tour of Europe

Left: Katherine's adopted daughter, Marie Christine
Right: Katherine and John Pratt in Hollywood, 1953

Then Katherine bought
a house in Haiti.
She loved that beautiful land.
She and John adopted
Marie Christine, a child
from another island.

But Katherine had no time
to rest in her new home.
She still needed money.
She still had to dance.

Sometimes her pain
and her money problems
made Katherine hard
to get along with.

A dancer's life
is hard work.
Here Katherine
relaxes in her
dressing room.

At last she had
to close her school.
After a rough trip
to the Far East,
she broke up
her dance company, too.

No more dancing,
thought Katherine.
Now she could live
in Haiti with her family
and get some rest.

Katherine Dunham watches a dance she made up for the movie *Green Mansions*.

Chapter 5

Another Home

Of course, Katherine
didn't stop working.
She loved dancing
too much to do that.

So she wrote
books about her life.
She made up dances for
different kinds of shows.

Katherine teaching at Southern Illinois University

She and John went to
Southern Illinois University
to make up more dances.
While they were there,
Katherine visited
East St. Louis, Illinois.

It was a terrible
place, across the
Mississippi River
from St. Louis,
Missouri.

Most people in
East St. Louis
were black and
very poor. Crime
was everywhere.
Many buildings
had burned or
were boarded up.

Katherine at her desk in
the Katherine Dunham Museum
in East St. Louis, Illinois

Just the place for a school,
thought Katherine.
But starting it wasn't easy.
So she got young people
in the city to help her.
She also moved there herself.

41

Vanoye Aikens has been a long-time friend and dance partner of Katherine. Above: They practice an acrobatic tango for a performance in Paris in 1951. Right: Vanoye and Katherine in 1987

At first, the school
taught judo, dancing,
and African drumming.
It also taught young people
better ways to think and live.

Now the school is
over twenty years old.
It has sent fine dancers
into the world.
It has made life better
for many people
in East St. Louis.

Glory Van Scott and
Vanoye Aikens performing
"Rites de Passage," one
of Katherine's dances

Katherine at a news conference in 1992. She was fasting to protest the way the United States government treated people from Haiti.

Katherine Dunham is
over 80 years old.
She uses a wheelchair.
But she still stays busy.

And in her heart
and in her many students,
Katherine still dances.

Important Dates

1910	June 22—Born in Glen Ellyn, Illinois, to Fanny and Albert Dunham
1914	Family moved to Joliet, Illinois
1927	Moved to Chicago
1930	Began first dancing school
1935	Went to West Indies
1940	Married John Pratt The Dunham Dance Company gave first show in New York City
1944	Began the Katherine Dunham School of Dance, New York City
1947–50	Toured Mexico, Europe, and Latin America with Dunham Dance Company
1952	Adopted Marie Christine
1954	Closed school in New York City
1956–57	Toured Australia, New Zealand, and Far East

1957	Disbanded the Dunham Dance Company
1967	Began the Performing Arts Training Center, East St. Louis, Illinois
1992	Began a fast to draw attention to Haitians who were refused entry to the United States

INDEX

Page numbers in boldface type indicate illustrations.

Africa, 20, 21
Aikens, Vanoye, **42**, **43**
arthritis, 33
Aunt Lulu, 7
ballet, 21
black dancing, 19, 20, 21, 23, 24, 25
books, 39
Chicago, Illinois, 7, 14, **15**, 16
college, 14, 15
Cousin Irene, 7
dance company, **22**, 25, 26, **26**, 27, **28**, 29, **29**, 30, **32**, 34, **34**, 37, **42**, **43**
dancing, 7, 10, 11, 13, 17, 19, 20, 21, 24, 25, 26, 29, 33, 34, 36, 37, 39, 44
dancing lessons, 11, 13, 16
dancing schools, 19, 20, 21, 33, 34, 37, 41, 43
dry-cleaning business, 9
Dunham, Albert, 5, **6**, 8, 14, **14**, 15, 17
Dunham, Annete, 8, **9**, 14
Dunham Dance Company, 27, 29, 34
Eagle Eye Society, 10
East St. Louis, Illinois, 40, **41**, 43
Europe, 34
Far East, 37
father of Katherine Dunham, 5, 7, 8, 11, 13, 14

Haiti, 23, 35, 37
high school, 13
Illinois, 26
Joliet, Illinois, 8
Latin America, 34
library, 15
Marie Christine, 35, **35**
Mexico, 34
Mississippi River, 41
money problems, 20, 34, 36
mother of Katherine Dunham, 5, 6, **6**
music, 5
New York City, 27, **27**, 33
operations, 33
pictures of Katherine Dunham, 2, **9**, **11**, **12**, **16**, **17**, **18**, **21**, **25**, **26**, **28**, **29**, **31**, **32**, **34**, **35**, **36**, **37**, **38**, **40**, **41**, **42**, **44**, **45**
Pratt, John, 25, **25**, 27, 35, **35**
St. Louis, Missouri, 41
school, 9, 10
secret club, 10
singing, 7, 10
Southern Illinois University, 40, **40**
sports, 13
theater, 7, 16
West Indies, 23

ABOUT THE AUTHOR

Carol Greene has degrees in English literature and musicology. She has worked
in international exchange programs, as an editor, and as a teacher of writing.
She now lives in Webster Groves, Missouri, and writes full-time. She has
published more than 100 books, including those in the Rookie Biographies
series.